Stop Whining And Start Winning!

The 7-Step Formula for Reaching All Your Goals

Paul C. Trottier

ISBN: 978-1-77277-065-0

Published by:
10-10-10 Publishing
Markham, ON
Canada

*I dedicate this book to my amazing family. Without
the support of my beautiful wife Tina, and the
loving push from my children, Brandon and Jordan,
this book would never have come into existence.
Thank you for inspiring me to always push myself
further and harder!*

*Also, to the memory of my parents; Paul senior and
Anne. I'm so grateful to have been blessed by their
hard work ethics and tenacity.*

FOREWORD

The *Stop Whining and Start Winning* teachings of Paul Trottier give you the blueprint to help you not only set goals, but to actually reach them! Inside this book, Paul walks you through his 7 step formula using his unique "DO DAILY™" technique. You wouldn't take a trip without first planning out the route, why should plotting your life's course be any different?

This book takes you to the core of your inner gifts, and shows you how to share your message with the world. Learn to bring your big goals back to life in a step-by-step plan to ensure your goals transpire to reality.

Throughout the book, Paul breaks down the DO DAILY™ acronym into steps that are easy to understand, apply and remember. *Stop Whining and Start Winning* is put together in a fun to read style.

If you are serious about your personal development, and reviving those dead dreams of yesterday into goals of today, then you have to read this book. You will never get stuck in reaching your goals again!

Raymond Aaron

New York Times Bestselling Author

ACKNOWLEDGEMENTS

I want to thank my parents who have instilled in me strong values, good work ethics, and drive to always do better. Although they have left this earth a number of years back, their thoughts remain with me daily. My mother, who was widowed much too early; and left to raise a family of seven, is my true hero! Her discipline and passion has gifted my character.

I want to thank my loving wife, Tina. She is my best friend, and has been my loyal cheerleader from day one. Her contagious smile has fueled my inspiration to finish this book.

My brother Ken and my eldest son Brandon helped with the special editing touches. For that I am forever grateful. They both have the vision of putting it all together.

And lastly, a special thank you to Raymond Aaron, and his ever professional team. Seeing how committed Raymond is, with regards to bringing out the very best for his students, ignited my passion to write this book in the first place. His guidance, wisdom and support helped me so much. Thank you all for your commitment to seeing me through this big project!

x

CONTENTS

INTRODUCTION:

I'm sure at some point you felt like you've hit a brick wall when it came to reaching your goals. It is much easier to quit and give up on a goal than to actually manifest your goal into reality.... Or is it? I think the main obstacle in reaching your goals, is that most people see their goals as sooo big; they just have no idea where to start. Also, there is really no game plan in place on exactly how they will reach that goal.

As the old proverb states; How *do you eat an elephant?* Answer; *One bite at a time!* That is the same theory in reaching your goals as well. Just chunk that big enormous goal down into smaller attainable goals, and you will see that big goal come to life faster than you can imagine!

It pains me to see so many people struggling in their day to day lives. It hurts me to see people feel as though they have to settle for mediocrity. Seriously, life is meant to be abundant, and you should be able to tap into some of that abundance! You doubt me? OK, allow me to prove it to you?

Let's have a closer look at nature around us. Let's take a single apple for example. Inside, one apple contains fifteen to twenty seeds. Each one of those seeds equals a tree. That's twenty fruit bearing trees. Each one of those twenty trees produces hundreds of branches, and each one of those branches produces thousands of buds that will develop into ripe and delicious apples. Every one of those thousands of apples per tree has fifteen to twenty seeds.... and thus, the cycle starts all over again! Season after season the abundance cycle of nature continues.

Do you still believe that there is not enough abundance for you to have your share? I certainly hope not! There is a step by step formula for reaching your goals and becoming successful, and I'm going to teach those steps to you in this book. Strap on your seatbelts; it's going to be a wild ride!

Before we go any further, you may be asking yourself 'Who is this Paul Trottier guy, and why does he think he's able to teach me about goals?' That's a fair question, so let me take a minute to introduce myself to you, so that you are a bit more comfortable and familiar with what this book has to offer.

I was born in Northern Ontario, Canada, in the mining town of Sudbury. I was the youngest of a humble family of seven, and although we never lacked any love in our household, there was always a struggle with the finances. I'm not really sure how my Mom and Dad supported a family of seven most of the time, but their dedication and hard work always seemed to pay off. Dad was a bar manager, which meant he worked nights, and slept during the days, so there wasn't really much father and son time. Mom was a home maker that was the glue of the family, and in essence, raised seven kids on her own. We learned to make do with what we had. I remember as a kid, mom cutting out the Styrofoam container from a package of ground hamburger to act as insoles to put in my boots, so they would last a few extra months... That's no joke! Now you understand why I used the description 'humble'!

Growing up in this small northern town, I did a number of jobs as a young adult to survive. My mom grew up on a farm, and was quick to instill good work ethics in her kids. "Never be ashamed of showing your working hands to anyone. It builds character!" was one of her favorite expressions.

One of my first jobs was actually my introduction to entrepreneurialism. I was fourteen, when my brother Ken, suggested that I go down to the nearby Drive-In and pitch them the idea of washing car windshields before the movies started. The owner of the Drive-In wouldn't even have to pay me. I would only take 'donations' from the drivers for what they thought my services were worth. At first, I thought my brother was nuts for even suggesting that idea!

"Think about this Paul" he would say. "If the owners of the Drive-In don't have to pay you; this means they'd probably be open to letting you do it, right? And if there is no expected price, most people would feel obligated to paying you at least a loonie (slang term for Canadian dollar). Each windshield would take you about 2 or 3 minutes to clean. That breaks down to about $30/hour of work!" Keep in mind, this was back in the early eighties... and I was only fourteen years old!! The truth was that most cars were paying me at closer to $2 or $3 for cleaning their windshields. I was making anywhere from $60 to $75 per hour. Or, to break it down further; I was coming home every night with anywhere from $120 to $150 cash in my pocket! My overhead; 2 jugs of windshield washer per week! I miss those days, indeed! I was earning more money at fourteen, then my first few years in the work force as an adult... tax free!

After high school, I decided my career path would be in hospitality. I did my schooling in North Bay, and then returned to my home city to begin my career journey. I worked various hospitality jobs including front desk at a Holiday Inn, assistant manager at Casey's and a 19th century themed banquet hall. They were all fun introduction jobs, but the hours were long, and the pay was minimal. At one point, I calculated my hourly rate as an assistant restaurant manager around the $7 per hour mark. Yikes!

By the late fall of 1998, I was unemployed, and living at my parent's summer camp. Both of my parents had passed on by this point, and since I was not earning ANY money, I was glad to have a roof over my head! Keep in mind; it was a roof and four walls, and not much more! The summer camp was not insulated. Nor did it have city water. My water supply came from a small piston pump that drew water to flush the toilet, but it wasn't drinkable. This water line was on the ground surface, meaning as soon as the temperature dropped below zero degrees Celsius, I no longer had <u>any</u> water supply. Late November in northern Ontario can get pretty cold... especially at night. Guess what? No furnace either! The camp was heated by a wood stove that had to be stoked up every few hours!

November 11th, 1998 is a date that I will always remember. I recall picking at my plate of canned beans, and doing my best to stay warm. My dominate thought was *"There is no way I'm going to survive through the winter in this place! My family is going to find me in the spring, frozen to death, inside our family camp!"* Just then, the phone rang and I snapped my out of my depressed thoughts. It was my sister Kathy who was working as a call coordinator for IBM in Southern Ontario. "Hey" she said. "They are looking for a backup parts person to work in the warehouse here. I think you'd be perfect for it, and you're welcome to stay with us until you get on your feet."

Humm. Let me see. I'm currently unemployed; I have about $50 to my name. I'm living in a summer camp that is more like a meat cooler (no offence mom and dad)... with no running water, barely able to afford groceries... What do you think my reply was? **"HELL YA I'M INTERESTED!!"** I sent in my resume, and by Nov 29th of that same year I was working my first real job since graduating from college. The pay was good (not great). I had a warm bed to sleep in and food in my fridge to eat when I was hungry!

It didn't take long to start earning enough money to finally get my own apartment, and begin feeling human again! And it could only get better! My future wife to be; lived about twenty minutes away! She was actually just getting separated from a guy that I went to high school with. It's a long story, but that's how I met her. Oh well, his loss is my gain!!

Although I was grateful to have a steady paycheck, and live in a home that was actually insulated, with a real furnace and running water... I soon realized that I was working much too hard for the bland paycheck that I was bringing home. As is the case with anyone working a J.O.B (just over broke), I knew I was working much too hard for my minuscule weekly paycheck. I was doing the hour long commute to and from work daily, and going home stressed and depressed.

I was sure there was a better way to support my family, and I was determined to figure it out. After numerous seminars, and years of procrastination, I was getting sick and tired of being sick and tired, and thus the *"Stop Whining and Start Winning"* book was born. I turned my mindset around and believed that I would not stop until I reached my goals. With the help of great mentors such as Raymond Aaron and Loral Langemeier, I discovered there is a systematical way of reaching my goals. This book is a collaboration of the system that I share with you today! No more whining about how bad things are; only an attitude adjustment and celebration of your accomplishments. Goals ACHIEVED!

Speaking of the rat trap grind that most people settle with, I'm often perplexed as to why most people feel that they have no other choice. Do you really feel that your self-worth is so low that you will need to succumb to the rat-trap cycle? I would hope not. What exactly is the rat-trap? Well, as I explained earlier... it is a long depressing road with no promising signs of it ever getting better.

Do you know anyone (perhaps intimately) who lives the life I'm about to describe? The alarm clock goes off much too early, and you roll over and smack the snooze button with frustration. Maybe you're a chronic snooze button whacker, and smack that annoying button many, many times! You haul your sorry butt into the shower, and can't get today's upcoming meeting out of your head, knowing your unappreciative boss is going to rake you over the coals. You sit in traffic for an hour or more and you right leg is numb doing the constant brake and accelerator pedal dance.

You finally get to work 40 minutes late and have to explain to you beady-eyed boss why it took you so long to get in. The daily grind continues with babysitting grown adults and typical office politics.

Finally, the clock hits the liberating 5 o'clock mark, and it's the first burst of energy you've had all day! You sprint out of the office to your car, only to find yourself shortly thereafter fighting the same traffic you had to deal with during the morning commute in!

By the time you get home, it's quarter past seven in the evening. Great... just enough time to wolf down some cold dinner and then numb yourself in front of the TV watching some pathetic reality shows while putting down a few dulling alcoholic beverages. You crash by about 11:00PM... knowing in a few short hours you get up to do it all over again!! Yeah!

Let us not forget the weekend either. Finally, you get a chance to lie back on your hammock and chill out for a few days, right? Wrong! There are the dreaded house chores that suck up about three quarters of your weekend. Everything from run the kids to their soccer game to cleaning up the house to mowing the lawn. Let's not forget the obligated visit to the in-laws as well. Great... a two-hour lecture how you are such an incompetent parent and blah, blah, blah! It's no wonder that 97% of the population are walking around like zombies, looking like they are about to strangle the first person that crosses them! If all of this sounds way too familiar, then I want to help you change that pattern starting today! Fair enough? Good!

As I've already mentioned, two of the main reasons why most people don't reach their goals is because your goals just seems too overwhelming, and also you don't have it planned out. It seems strange to me that most people will spend weeks or months planning out their two week vacation, but won't take fifteen minutes to put a plan together to reach their *life* goals! Part of your goal plan is to chunk your big scary monster-like goals down into smaller attainable steps. Do you think you can say, *"My goal is to start a brand new business tomorrow, and by the end of the week, be earning $100,000 per month?"* Sorry to burst your bubble, but not very likely that will happen... at least not without a very solid plan.

You wouldn't even consider getting in the car to travel some place you've never been without looking on MapQuest, pulling out your GPS or even (for you non techie people), unfolding the dusty map in the glove compartment and figuring out your best option to get to your **destination**.

That is exactly what you need to do to reach your goals as well. Your plan will tell you where you are now... where you want to be to reach your destination... and your best route to get you there. Did you know that roughly 93% of people who just make the effort to write down their goals actually reach them? But sadly, only a very small percent of the population even do that much. As long as your goals stay in your head, and never get down on paper that you can review daily, your odds of reaching those goals drops dramatically!

Planning it Out

You may have heard of the **S.M.A.R.T** technique for reaching your goals (Specific, Measurable, Attainable, Realistic, and Timely). I will go into more details further on in this book, but for now let's just understand that it works! It is a tried and true path to your success.

The **S.M.A.R.T** technique overlaid with my **D.O. D.A.I.L.Y** ™ technique (Delegate, Offer Help, De-clutter, Apply your knowledge, Increase Happiness, Learn something new, Yearn for the reward), is a guaranteed sure way for you to stop wishing and hoping your dreams and goals might happen , and actually start living your goals in the present! Can you imagine? No more sitting on the side-lines watching other people meet their goals, while you watch yet another year go by without meeting any of your goals. Those days are gone my friend. I'm excited to walk you through this powerful formula!

Have you ever noticed the drastic difference between your rear view mirror, and your front windshield? This may sound like a strange question, but let's seriously consider this for a moment. The average rear view mirror is about two inches by five inches. It is a reflection of where you have just been, right? How about the front windshield of your car? The average size for most windshields is about 3 feet by 6 feet. Do you think it was a fluke that it worked out that way, or did the car engineers plan it that way on purpose? Quite obviously, this is an intentional design of the car. But, the question is why?

Simply put, the designers of the car want you to put a large amount of your attention and focus on where you are **going**, and very little attention on where you have **been**! Read that sentence again, it's that important! You're probably thinking to yourself by now 'what do car windshields and rear view mirrors have to do with reaching my goals?' In a word... plenty!

I'm sure you've talked to people who are frozen in their tracks with fear about whether or not they will be able to reach their goals. They have a really hard time envisioning their future goals, because for the most part, they never were able to reach these goals in the past. They keep saying to themselves 'well, my bank account has never been higher than $___ (whatever your figure is)... How can I possible break that financial ceiling now?' or 'How am I supposed to start my own business? I've never done anything like that!' A few of my favorite lines are 'There is no way I could ever reach that goal... I'm just too___ (old/ overweight/ not smart enough/ don't have any contacts). Whatever lame excuse you have, toss it in the trash can right now will you? It's no more than a bunch of poppy cock! There is no way you will ever reach your dream goals while you are looking in your rear view mirror of life. You need to put your focus on the big, bright future that lies ahead of you in front of your windshield of life!

The sooner you can learn to unplug those debilitating and limiting beliefs, and plug into empowering, strong and positive beliefs, the sooner you will be reaching your goals, and the sooner you will be living the glorified life you dream about! Your mind is your strongest arsenal in your tool bag to reach your goals. I will show you how to use your thinking to work in your favor. I believe in you, and soon enough, you will believe in your own natural abilities as well. Let's do this!

Alright, all ready. I hear you! I know you've had enough motivation talk, and you're fired up to get to the goods and learn how you can change your ways to a better and happier life! I'm just as pumped to teach you the 7-step formula that will turn your life around starting today, and you will soon see all of your goals manifesting before your very eyes! It's important that we cover the basics and get you in the right mind set before digging into the meat and potatoes of this program.

What would happen if you took an exotic sports car like a Ferrari, and put low grade, watered down gas in the engine? You'd probably get some sputtering and spitting and have a hard time to get it out of first gear. A car like a Ferrari needs to be finely tuned and can only run to its maximum performance with the best fuel. You are my Ferrari, my friend. There is no way I would even think of taking a Ferrari out of the driveway unless it was running in top condition, with the highest octane fuel and synthetic oil in the engine!

Follow what I'm saying? You are a magnificent machine that may not have had the proper maintenance it needed to be at optimal running condition. I want to polish this brilliant sports car to a fine gloss shine. I want to put only the best gas and oil in this amazing machine. I want to make sure all the tires are filled with the optimum pressure of nitrogen. Only when I know this fabulous beast of machinery is primed and ready, inside and out, will I take it out and push it for the results I know it can achieve!

We are about to embark on a great adventure together. But be warned: This will be an adventure where I will push your buttons and force you to feel a bit uncomfortable at times. Can you recall that uncomfortable feeling as a child when your shoes were too small for your growing feet? Well maybe you have outgrown some of your old mind sets. I suspect you will not like me as much as you do now, while I push you through this 7-step formula. But understand this. I will push you because I believe in you!

I do promise you this; stick with me, and by the time we complete this success adventure, you will be thanking me. And you will wish you had read this book much sooner. We are going to take the last few decades of misguided and infested information that has polluted your thinking and replace it with the success formula you are now learning. Get ready to surprise yourself, because you won't believe how fast and easy it is to reach your goals, when you follow my 7-step formula! Are you ready? Good, me too!

<u>AH-HA NOTES!</u>

_____

_____

_____

_____

_____

_____

_____

_____

_____

_____

_____

_____

_____

_____

Step 1: <u>**D**ELEGATE</u>

(**D**O DAILY™)

"Focus on your strengths; delegate your weaknesses!"

-Author Unknown

Relating back to the introductory chapter, I explained that when you combine the SMART formula in reaching your goals (Specific, Measurable, Attainable, Realistic and Timely), combined with my DODAILY™ technique, the first step is to delegate. That statement may shake you a bit, as you might be thinking, 'I don't know how to delegate and lead people' or 'I'm a lone ranger... I don't need anyone to help me reach my goals'. I'm sorry to say, but that is just your self-limiting beliefs that will only keep you stuck. There is no such thing as a self made millionaire. Every successful person has a team that helps them reach their goals more accurately, in less time, with less stress!

Let's talk in detail about who you want to have as part of your dream team! There are a number of key people you will need to help you reach your goals. Before we talk about who you need on your dream team, let's cover who NOT to incorporate into your dream team: Family members (there, I said it). We all have them. But if we are honest, some family members, while possibly trying to protect you... only destroy your positive mindset attitude and crush your confidence in reaching your goals. They often dream small, and play 'not to lose'. In fact though, you need people around you that dream outside the box, and play the game of life to win. Do you see the difference? One is a negative mindset, where they don't ever step out of their comfort zone to reach their goals. The other is a group that believes in themselves, and believes in you. They are willing to get uncomfortable to reach their goals, and take calculated steps to get there. Unsuccessful poor people will say 'I can't afford it', whereas wealthy, goal oriented people will say 'How can I afford it?' Big difference in mindset, wouldn't you agree?

I've always been puzzled by how most people will talk to less successful, low ambition people for their advice on how to better their lives.   How many conversations between two co-workers at the water cooler have you overheard that sounded something like this?

Joe: "Hi Mary.. I'm thinking about going after my life-long goal of writing a book, and starting my own business. What do you think?"

Mary: "Are you serious Joe? Writing a book is so much work, and time consuming!   Besides, you've never written a book... what makes you think you can do something like that? I doubt you have the ability to do anything like that. As far as starting your own business... come on! You aren't the entrepreneur type! Again, that is a lot of work, and I'm sure you have no idea on what is needed to run a successful business. Besides, I've heard that 95% of small businesses fail after the first eighteen months! Those are bad ideas, Joe. I wouldn't suggest it..."

Joe: "Humm. Yeah, I guess you're right Mary. I don't know what I was thinking. Thanks for pointing me in the right direction."

And there you have it. In less than a one minute conversation, Joe's goals are crushed and halted even before he puts a plan together to go for it! First of all, why would Joe present his idea to a co-worker who doesn't give a hoot about his goals? Mary is just a fellow 'play-not-to-lose' co-worker. Most likely she has never written a book, nor even thought about starting her own business! If you want to grow, and go for goals that are going to stretch you, wouldn't it make more sense to talk to someone that has already achieved your goal, and can mentor you on the best way to actually reach your goal? Do you think when I wrote this book, I asked someone who has never written a book for help? Or did I seek out someone who has written many books to be my mentor and help me get started? Learn from a master! You must be wondering, 'well then who you do I want to be part of my dream building team, Paul? I'm glad you asked!

There are so many key people you need on your team. But for some perplexing reason, most people never enlist help when trying to reach your goals. There probably are a dozen or so reasons. I suspect one of the main reasons is money- or lack thereof. They feel that hiring the expert personnel they need to reach their goals is going to cost them too much money.

I prefer to look at this from the other side of the coin. How much time and money are you or your business going to *lose* if you don't have a professional team guiding you to your goals in a stress free and timely fashion?

Some of the key people you want on your dream team include (but not limited to) mentors, coaches, home support, expert support, and as I said earlier, someone who has already blazed the trail for whatever you want to achieve!

Let's talk about starting a business for example. You are going to be expected to give up some of your time and money to reach that goal, right? So what you need to ask yourself is, 'How do I get more time, and earn more money?' The secret is what I've said all along. You get a team! Are you someone that cleans your own house? Most non-goal oriented people will say of course I clean my own home, but those on a mission to reach their goals, will say they can't possibly reach their goals *without* a home support team!

Think about it. **Every week** you and your partner spend an average of 15-20 hours cleaning and organizing your home. Add up all you do around your home, and you will see that number is pretty accurate, even conservative! Don't forget the time doing laundry, folding, ironing, yard work, grocery shopping, car maintenance and home repairs. That is precious time you are robbing from yourself every week that could actually be used for reaching your goals! I'd like you to ponder which option is hurting you more.

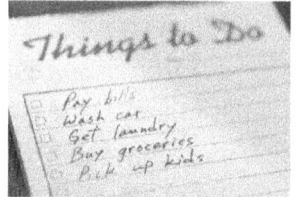

Let's say you hire a cleaning person at $15 per hour. That would be $225 per week. You're first reaction may be 'That's a lot of money... I can't afford that!' What would the high-achieving goal setting person say? Remember... "How <u>can</u> I afford that, so that I get 15-20 hours of my time back?"

How about this... you take that 15-20 hours per week, and create an on-line digital product that you can sell over and over again. That digital product sells for a $75 profit. That means you would only need to sell a minimum of 3 of these products per week to cover the cost of hiring a cleaning person for your home! Chances are though, that if you create a product that the market really wants, you will be selling much more than three per week, AND still come home to a nice clean home AND have 15-20 hours per week of your time back!

Why is it that so many new entrepreneurs feel that they have to be Jack of many trades, and master of none? Perhaps you are a small business owner, and you are the one that markets your product or service, creates the invoices, cleans the office toilets, submits the taxes, and everything in between. Two problems arise here. First, you are not an expert in all those fields, and second, trying to wear all hats, only drains your time and energy!

A life coach, like myself, can help you create a similar plan, and get you on track to start living your dream life. Please see the back of the book for a special offer on how I can help you turn your dreams into reality!

<u>AH-HA NOTES!</u>

_____

_____

_____

_____

_____

_____

_____

_____

_____

_____

_____

_____

_____

_____

Step 2: **O**FFER HELP!

(D**O**DAILY™)

"You can get everything in life you want
if you will just help enough other people get what they want."
- Zig Ziglar, Motivational Speaker

Let me tell you about a *friend* I had when I was a boy. One Christmas morning my *friend* got up and ran downstairs to open his gifts. He opened the first gift, and was shocked to see that it was the same gift they got him last year. 'Hey!' he exclaimed...'It must be a mistake.' He opened his second gift. 'Hey!' he shrieked. 'They got me this gift last year too!' Third gift..'Hey!' fourth gift.. 'Hey!'

The little boy ran upstairs to his mother's bedroom and woke her up. 'Mama, mama' he said. 'All my Christmas gifts are the exact same gifts from last year. You just took last year's gifts, rewrapped them, and gave them back to me again!' His mother looked kindly into his eyes and said 'Son, that's because you never **used** last year's gifts. Use the gifts you already have, and then you will get more!' Wow! That was the deepest lesson my friend ever had. That friend was me!

Would you agree with me that most of the population doesn't appreciate selfish people? True? Then why are you being such a selfish person and not sharing your gifts with others?! Don't take that statement the wrong way. I'm not saying that you eat the whole box of cookies by yourself, or take up three seats on the morning bus ride. What I am saying is that each and every one of us has a special gift inside that they are not sharing with the world. This isn't necessarily because they choose not to share their gift, but more likely because they don't believe their gift is of any value!

Remember in the previous chapter how we talked about having a strong team to help you reach your goals? This is what I mean about sharing your unique gift with the world! Most people believe that they only have 2 or 3 skills they are good at. You should be focusing on those 2 or 3 skills you do well, and leave the rest of those specialized skills that you do not have, to those who excel at those skills. I don't understand why so many small business entrepreneurs feel they have to wear all the hats in their business.

I have never flown a 747 jumbo jet or performed open heart surgery. I would never in a million years even attempt to do either one of those things unless I had years of training, education and experience behind me. Why then, will someone who is aiming for their big goals think they can do a better job at cleaning their home and managing their own books? Why do they think they can reach all of their goals without the support of a coach and someone to show them the path? Why would you even want to? Really... I don't like cleaning my home (I don't think the average person does either), nor am I very good at it. It takes me twice as long, never sparkles like it does when done professionally, and eats up valuable time I don't have! Why would you NOT want to bring in a home support member to help you with this task? And here's the thing... the person that supports my family and I by cleaning our home, and taking care of us... they are providing **their unique gift** to us. You all have a special talent and/or skill inside of you, which if shared with others, would make this world that much better!

Perhaps you've heard of the four different levels of exchange. It is important realize the differences between these levels, so that you will know where you stand in your own business.

1. **Criminal** – When you take something and don't pay for it, or worse, you offer your services or products to others without asking them to pay. They will never put any value on what you have given them. Why should they... you certainly haven't!

2. **Partial** – When you promise to deliver a product or service to a customer that has paid you, but you don't deliver the full product that the customer has paid for. For example, you go to the salon and pay for a haircut and blow dry, but only get the haircut. You, the customer, feels cheated, and may very well not return

3. **Fair** – When you provide exactly what was promised for the compensation agreed upon.

You go to the store and pay one dollar for a pack of gum, and the clerk gives you the gum.

4. **Exchange in Abundance** – When you provide something that is unexpected and unrelated to what was purchased. This is not more of what they have already paid for. (Example: you order a one scoop ice cream cone, and they give you two scoops). Rather what I mean is you get Wowed by getting an extra bonus! (Example: you order a plain one scoop ice cream cone, and they give it to you in a sugar cone, with sprinkles and chocolate sauce!)

'Exchange in Abundance' is what you want to aim for in your business, so that you will stand out among the crowd. Think of ways you can go beyond regular fair exchange so you can leave a memorable impression with your clients.

Another pet peeve of mine is those who do share their unique gift with others, but refuse to put any value on their special talent or inner gift. I'm sure at some point; you have freely given your unique gift to friends and family, without even thinking of asking for anything in return. When you provide a service or product to someone without them paying for it, in essence, you are allowing them to be a thief! Seriously! You don't always have to exchange your unique gift for money, but there should be equal exchange of services.

For example, my wife runs a lawn care maintenance company during the summer months. We usually take a trip to my home city to catch up with my siblings and extended family. We have a great arrangement with one of our regular customers, who just

happens to run a dog sitting business out of her home. We have a dog that needs to be looked after while we are gone, and she has a yard that needs TLC care. Although neither one of us ever pay for each other's services, we never expect to give our gifts out for free either. Instead, we exchange our own unique service gifts to each other. We clean up her yard and flower gardens, and get them looking amazing, and in exchange, she is happy to care for our black lab dog for a few days while we are away visiting family. It's called the Barter System and it's as old as time.

You all have a special gift inside of you. It is time to open up and share that gift with others, and never sell yourself short! There is value in what you have to share with the world. Please don't make the mistake that most of the world do where they under-value their special gift. You have a skill or service that others don't, and they are willing to pay you for it! It's time to share your gifts!

If you think about it, you will see that it is a precise and concise circle of life. You have your inner gifts that many people are happy to have you share with them. At the same time, there are things that others are much better at, which you need to incorporate into your life. If we all open up and share our gifts, the power of many comes into existence.

<u>AH-HA NOTES!</u>

_____

_____

_____

_____

_____

_____

_____

_____

_____

_____

_____

_____

_____

_____

_____

_____

Step 3:<u>De-clutter</u>

(DODAILY™)

"Until the clutter is cleared from your life,

the clarity will always remain cloudy!"

- Paul C. Trottier, Author and Transformation Coach

Are you like so many people out there that have a cluttered, unorganized mess in just about every corner of your home? What about your home office, or your bedroom? Are there excess papers on the desk, or a pile of cloths to be put away? Do you have gum wrappers and fast food packaging in the backseat of your car? I hate to be the one to tell you this, but all those unappealing piles of clutter and dirt are killing your chances of reaching your dreams! You ask me ... Paul, do you mean to tell me that if everything around me is cluttered and messy, that I will have a hard time attaining my goals? Yes, that is exactly what I'm saying!! Every mess in your life is a locked door that is keeping abundance out! Your inspiration, focus and passion get depleted with every mess in your life, and your negative thoughts and self doubt increase!

I want you to pay attention to what your emotions are telling you every time you walk into a cluttered room in your home. You may not even realize it, but I can be pretty sure that your immediate reaction is 'Argh... I hate seeing this mess every time I walk into this room!' Your energy level just gets sucked out of you before you even know it! Don't believe me? OK, picture this: You are celebrating a special night with your better half, and decide to splurge and rent the best suite at the Royal Hilton. You walk into the suite, and everything is prestigious and organized. The bathroom sparkles like diamonds; the towels are crisp clean white and aligned perfectly. The bed is made with love, with the throw cushions placed just right. The sun is shining through spotless windows, and the room is elegantly decorated, and inviting. Alright, how are you feeling right at this moment? I'd be willing to guess that your inner self is saying something like 'Wow... That's marvelous! What a fantastic room!' You are enlightened, and your energy level just went up a few notches! You can't tell me a clutter-free; welcoming environment like that doesn't empower a person!

I'm not going to be a hypocrite and say that I have this part of the DO DAILY ™ process totally under control. In fact, I'll be the first to tell you this step is a daily challenge for me. But, I will tell you this. I've been making a conscious effort to make sure my environment is as tidy and clutter-free as possible. It used to drive me nuts when I'd wake up, stumble into the kitchen to put the coffee on, and be greeted with a sink and counter full of dirty dishes! I tried to ignore that mess, but it would haunt me throughout the day. Every time I went to the kitchen for a drink of water or quick snack, I'd see the mess of dishes, and could feel my blood pressure rise, and my energy level deplete! After attending a few seminars with the same speaker... saying the same thing about how a messy environment will drain your positive energy... I figured, what do I have to lose? I'm going to take his advice and see what happens.

Before I go to bed, I make sure that the kitchen is spotless. Mind you, I mumble and grumble while I'm cleaning it up, and say things to myself, 'Why am I the only one in the family who cleans this kitchen? Why don't my kids or wife help tidy up this room?' By the time I'm done, the kitchen looks great, and I go to sleep peacefully. Now, when I wake up and go to the kitchen to put the coffee on, I smile as I walk into the kitchen and say to myself 'Oh yeah baby! It's going to be an awesome day!" And you know what? Most of the time, just by declaring that statement in the morning... it turns out to be just that! Who knew? Well, I guess my mentor, Raymond Aaron, actually knows what he's talking about!

It's not only physical messes in your environment that suck the life out of you. Open cycles will do the exact same thing? What are open cycles you ask? Well, let me ask you this. How efficient is your computer when you have a dozen or more applications all open at the same time? Your computer slows down significantly and becomes sluggish, right? Your brain operates the same way when you have too many things on the go with open cycles. Let's say you are driving down a busy freeway, talking on the phone to someone about a problem at work, thinking of what you need to pickup for your son's birthday party, remember you have to pay the phone bill when you get home, stop for gas on the way home and realize your library book is a week late to be returned!

My head is spinning just typing that out! Can you imagine being in that scenario? The sad truth is that there are so many people living this crazy, busy life style daily. It's no wonder they can't get focused and start manifesting their goals!

You need to close off as many open cycles in a day as you possibly can. The simplest way of doing this of course, is to put all your 'to do' items for the day in a calendar, manual or electronic, it doesn't matter. If you have four things that need to be done today, write them down on a list. Then, study the list and number them 1 to 4. The first item is your most important task to do that day. You don't do the second task until the first task is done. Your least important task for the day is the last item you do, number four. That way, you are getting your most important, goal oriented tasks done first. The most pressing open cycles get closed off every day. Remember to ask yourself prior to doing a task, 'Is this use of my time moving me closer to my goal, or further from it?' Sound simple? It is. You just have to be open and willing to try it. We all have the same 24 hours per day. Why is that some people (usually most successful) are always calm and cool, and seem to have excess time on their hands? And there are others that just never seem to have enough time in the day? It's all about how you manage your daily tasks. You can spend it watching mindless TV, or you can spend it being productive. Instead of spending 2-3 hours per night watching TV or doing mindless tasks, how about using that time to better yourself and work towards reaching your goals?

I'm a strong believer that your environment creates your future. There is a fish in Japan, called a Koi fish. If you take this fish and put him in one of those small, single fish bowls... give him all the food and water it wants... The Koi fish will never grow more than a few inches in size. But, if you take that same fish, take him out of that tiny fish bowl, and throw him into an open pond where he can swim around in... that Koi fish will now grow to about twelve inches in length! The question is- Why? The answer is simple. The Koi fish will grow in proportion to its environment. This is true for you, and it is true for me.

So, if you feel that you are trapped in a glass box, and not reaching your full potential, sit back and examine your environment. Who are you hanging around with?

Do you hang around whinny, negative people that bitch and complain all the time? If so, you yourself may be someone who feels like the victim that can never do any better.

The truth is that successful people hang out with people that are MORE successful then themselves. Why? The do this because they want to change their environment. If you have people around you that are successfully setting and manifesting their goals, do you think you are more or less likely to reach your goals? Obviously, you are compelled to play a bigger, better game when you hang around people that are already doing it! I encourage you to immerse yourself around people that are living the life, earning the income and reaching the goals that you want. Quickly, you will see your own life get turned around for the better... I promise!

<u>AH-HA NOTES!</u>

_____

_____

_____

_____

_____

_____

_____

_____

_____

_____

_____

_____

_____

Step 4: **Apply** your Knowledge

(DO DAILY™)

"Your time is limited, so don't waste it living someone else's life"
- Steve Jobs, Apple Founder

Did you know that about 67 percent of the population never read a nonfiction book once they are done their secondary or post secondary studies? Shocking, I know! I love reading nonfiction books about personal growth and how the mind works. I wasn't crazy about reading when I was in high school. The teachers picked the books I had to read and we had much different tastes in subject matter.

But as I got older, I appreciated the value of what the books had to offer. If you are reading this book, I would suspect you are like me, and enjoy learning new things to better yourself. Perhaps you also enjoy attending personal growth seminars. I've been to many, and just love sharing the high energy of the attendees, and taking notes of the wisdom shared by the speakers. I realized that I have many original ideas that I am sharing with you now.

My wife asked me why I went to so many seminars. I told her I got ignited with the passion in the air, and loved learning what the speakers were teaching me. 'Really?' she asked. 'Do you ever do anything with all this great information you are learning?' "Well, of course!" I replied enthusiastically. 'Really?' she shot back. 'Like what specifically?' Humm. I didn't have an answer for her.

Then she said something that really stuck with me. 'In fact, you have binders and binders of notes that you have taken from past personal growth seminars, but I've never once seen you even review the notes you have taken!' I hated to admit it, but she was right. I realized that I had a mental block that was stopping me from doing something positive with all this wonderful information I was learning! I did a personal check, and came to the conclusion that I was, in a way, a bit of a fraud. I was telling everyone I was a student of personal growth. But the reality was... I wasn't! It was time to step up to the plate and own it! It was time for me to start practicing what I was preaching, and take action to reach my big scary goals.

One of my biggest dreams was to write a book and share with you my years of personal growth information that was locked in my head. Isn't that nice of me? I admit it's scary at times, but at the same time, so empowering to be gifting this knowledge with you. Please don't make the same mistake I did and put this book on your shelf and never take action. "Shelf Help" books (not a typo) will never do you any good until you dive in head first! Don't be afraid. We will tackle any goal you want to reach, together. Fair enough?

I think—no, I know -- what it is that is stopping you from taking the needed actions to turn all the information in your brain into living the life of your dreams. Do you want to know what it is? You already know as well. The answer is fear. What is **fear**? False Evidence Appearing Real.

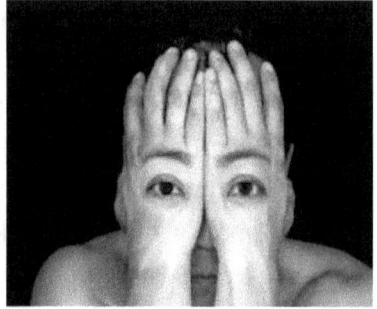

It is in essence, a lie that you are telling yourself. You feed the lie into your mind, and then believe it. Once you start believing your own lies, then your subconscious will do just about anything possible to stop you from actually reaching your goals.

Let's delve into where these lies that we tell ourselves daily actually come from. The fear you feel within, actually births from one of two places. Firstly, you are looking back at your life and comparing past goals to future goals you want to achieve. For example, if you have never earned more than $50,000 in a year... it's virtually impossible to picture earning $500,000 or more in a year. But the truth is that you can! There is no ceiling on the income you can earn. Only a limit on your beliefs of what you <u>think</u> you can earn. It is all mindset, and by the time you finish this book, I promise your beliefs will be stretched much further than you ever imagined. If you can see it, you can be it! Really! The other catalyst in this scenario is when your brain starts to ask the 'What if?' questions. You know what I mean don't you?

- "What if I go for this big goal, and fail?"
- "What will everyone think of me if I don't reach this goal?"
- "What if I succeed at reaching the goal, and change to a different person?"
- "What if I become an ass once I reach my goal?"
- "What if I become wealthy and everyone starts to pester me for money?"

All these outrageous questions can haunt you. But the truth is…. So what? I can promise you are going to have some rough spots on route to reaching your goals! How bad do you really want to reach that goal? That's what you have to keep asking yourself. Why is it important for you to reach your goal?

Remember when I said your mind will do just about anything to keep you from reaching your goal if you let your fear steer the ship? I want to challenge you to be aware of that voice that tries to talk you out of reaching your goals. When you say to yourself, "Right after dinner, I'm going to sit down and work on writing that book." Immediately after that you hear the evil second voice (your subconscious mind) says, 'You're no writer… might as well sit back and watch some TV.' Be aware of this voice and just ignore it. It's time for you to share the knowledge in your head and aim high for that amazing goal that you know will change your life!

I want to share a little exercise that one of my earlier mentors had me go through. I had large aspirations of the goals I wanted to achieve both professionally and personally. The problem was that my own self belief was that of fear. I couldn't even take the first step. My mentor saw this as a hurdle that I had to overcome, if I any hope of reaching my goals at all.

He introduced me to a little self challenging game called 'The Toothpick Trade Up'. Basically, I start off with a single toothpick that I got from my pantry. The whole point of this little challenge is to convince total strangers that what I had was of more value than what they had, and thus, do a trade up.

I knew this was going to be tough wrapping my head around, because let's face it... how much value can you put on a toothpick, right? I decided that I was going to play full out and see where it led to. I had to do at least three different trade-ups within a 24-hours span. Humm.... Where and how would I convince someone that my one cent toothpick was worth any value to them?

I started off the next morning at work. There were a number of co-workers sitting around the lunch table, when I noticed that the lady sitting across from me was trying to discretely remove something out of her teeth. I knew this was my chance. I looked at her, and said "It looks like you could use a toothpick, there." 'Yes' she replied, 'but I don't think they have any in the cafeteria.'

"Well, tell you what... I have a new toothpick here you can use. By the way, are you planning to eat that granola bar?"

'No', she replied 'I'm quite full.'

"How about this... I'll trade you this toothpick for your granola bar..."

'Sure, sounds great!' Wow! I did it. I made my first trade and got something of higher value for my toothpick. My heart raced, as I now knew it was possible.

Now, how would I craft my second trade-up? It was only a few hours later when the magic happened. I ventured into the Canadian Tire parking lot, and nervously looked for someone that seemed in need of a granola bar. I felt like a creepy stalker, but I finally noticed a man come out of the store with a few bags and a refreshing bottle of unopened cola. I approached him, and explained my training dilemma. He said he admired my sense of courage, and was willing to trade my granola bar for his large bottle of chilled Cola. I couldn't believe it! I started off with a one cent toothpick, and less than 12 hours later, I traded my way up to a $4.00 bottle of cola.

It was time for my last trade. My confidence had climbed exponentially! I knew by this point I could do this! Within minutes, another man came out of the store, carrying a few bags. I noticed sitting on the top of the bag, a pair of leather work gloves. I approached him with head high, and shoulders back.

"Excuse me sir… how are you today?"

'Fine…' he responded somewhat cautiously.

"Great! I'm conducting an experiment today, to see if people would be willing to trade an item in their possession for a refreshing bottle of Coke™".

'Really?' He seemed intrigued. 'What do you have in mind?'

"Well, I see you have a pair of garden gloves, there in your bag… what about that?"

'Sure, sounds good to me!' He replied immediately. "It's stinking hot out here today. I could use a nice cold soft drink right about now!"

And there it was. Done with ease, and virtually no insecurities on my part! I started this quest off as a scared, timid boy who was faced with the challenge of proving the value of a toothpick. A toothpick! How much value is there in a toothpick? By the end of this little confidence building challenge, I was a strong, confident man who knew I had value to offer the world! I increased my net value by over a thousand percent! Can you do this? You better believe it! In fact, I'd highly recommend you do!

<u>AH-HA NOTES!</u>

_____

_____

_____

_____

_____

_____

_____

_____

_____

_____

_____

_____

_____

Step 5: **Increase** your Happiness

(DO DAILY™)

"Happiness is a journey... not a destination!"

-*Ben Sweetland, author*

What is it that we all want more of in our life? Happiness, of course! I mean, isn't that why people set goals in the first place? You set a goal to go on that two week vacation to a hot tropical island, and lounge on the beach to feel happy! You set the goal to lose 15 pounds so that cute guy or gal at the gym may notice you! Thus, you feel happy. You set that goal to have a million dollars in your bank account to buy that wonderful lakefront home and fast sports car so that you feel happy! You set the goal to get married and have a family so that you feel happy! I can go on here, but I think you get the idea. We all want to live a wonderful happy and fulfilled life; but sadly, most people are dragging their sorry butts around living their life by default instead of desire! They are doing what they *have* to do to survive... not what they *want* to do to thrive!

As great as all these things sound, there is an underlying problem you may not even been seeing. Did you pick it up? All those examples I listed are just superficial things. Yes, they make you happy for a brief time, but will they ignite the passion within to keep you striving to be the best you could possibly be? Now, don't get me wrong. I'm not saying that aiming to have more in your life is a bad thing. Everyone wants to bring more rewards into their life, and as you should. What I am saying is that focusing on just superficial things will not likely keep you focused on your goals when the going gets tough down that path.

When you're planning to go for those big scary bodacious goals... you need to go much deeper than just the things that will make you happy for a short period of time. A lot of people will say that they want to bring wealth into their life. On the surface this sounds like a great goal to shoot for, but is it really what you want? At this point, I suggest you let your inner child come out to bring you to your true goal. The one word question that every toddler asks, that every adult hates to answer. "WHY?" I going to tell you never accept the first thing that comes to your mind as your ultimate goal. You need to ask yourself the intense 'why' question <u>at least three times</u> to really know what your big goal is.

You start off by saying 'I want more money in my life. I want to be rich!' That's a great first step, but **_why_** do you want more money? (That's #1)

'I want more money so I can quit my job and not worry about bills coming in.' Good... but **_why_** do you want to quit your job? (There's #2)

'Well, if I can quit my job, I can start my own business and work from home' Oh boy, now we are getting somewhere. That's great, but **_why_** would you possibly want to work from home? (There's #3)

'Well, I'd love to spend more time with my wife and kids, so we can travel the world together and learn different cultures of the world!'

Ah, now that's a goal that you will stay focused on reaching, no matter how rough things get along the way to reaching that big goal! If you just focus on the first stage of this goal- "I want to be rich" Sorry, but that just isn't deep enough or strong enough to pull you through the hard bumps along the way. Write down that true purpose goal. The answer to your third or fourth 'why' question, is the driving force that will keep you on track when the going gets tough. Read that deep rooted reason first thing in the morning and last thing before going to bed, and you will find that you won't quit until the goal is reached!

Have you ever noticed that when you wake up in a bad mood, you start feeling negative about the whole day? What happens? First you stub your toe as you get out of bed, then you scold yourself in the shower, and before you know it, you're involved in a 2-car fender bender, and 2 hours late for work!

What about when you wake up feeling *great*, and feel that you can handle any challenge that life tosses your way? The sun is shining, your kids give you a big hug as you drop them off at school, you're early for work and get a few 'to do' items knocked off before the big meeting. The customer loves your presentation, and decides to buy in to the solution you present to them. Life is awesome, and there is nothing going to stop you from reaching all of your goals! What's the difference? I'm sure you may have heard of the Law of Attraction, but not understand it in its entirety.

Let me see if I can break it down for you. The Law of Attraction says that in short, like attracts like. What you put most of your attention on every day, is what you will bring into your life. In the example above, the person that woke up in a bad mood, brought upon their own 'crappy day' so to speak. Perhaps they didn't intentionally think all those bad things were going to happen, but you can rest assured that those thoughts were in their subconscious mind! The same is true for the person that had a really good day. They may not have known it when they first woke up, but as each good event happened, their energy shift changed for the better.

When you see a successful person walk by, you may at first think "Wow, that person has all the luck". That's not true at all. The successful person is just better at managing their energy frequency. They focus on good things happening to them on a daily basis. In fact, they confidently believe it, and they know good things will just happen without question. Successful people have learnt to manage their biggest asset with intense precision. That asset of course is their mind! When you can confidently align your conscious mind and your subconscious mind, there is no goal that is untouchable! Wealthy, successful goal-oriented people know with rock solid certainty, that if they want a certain goal, all they need to do is believe and clearly envision it, while taking inspired action.

If you were listening to a radio station, and a song, or type of music came on that you didn't like, what would you do? Simply, walk over to the radio selector, and turn it to a station that you enjoy. Easy enough, right? You can do this in your life as well. If you are having a crappy day, and you don't like where your energy is at... without effort you can change your frequency. Tune your life into a higher energy, so that the pathway for your goals opens up for you. Align your energy with your deepest passion, and miracles will happen for you!

When you consciously focus on keeping your thoughts positive, you will see good things evolve right before your eyes! Seriously! Most people say 'I will believe it when I see it'. In actual fact, they should be saying **'I'll see it once I believe it!'**

In summary, when you feel your emotions take a turn for the worse, you can easily shift your energy and bring it back up again. All you need to do is think of something that makes you feel good. For me, it's wrestling with my boys, walking on the beach with my wife, my first kiss, crawling into bed with fresh sheets that just came out of the dryer, listening to my favorite song... You get the idea. Do that.

<u>AH-HA NOTES!</u>

_____

_____

_____

_____

_____

_____

_____

_____

_____

_____

_____

_____

_____

_____

Step 6: **Learn** Something New

(DO DAILY™)

"Education is the only thing that nobody can ever take away from you!"-Anne Petersen-Trottier, my wonderful mother

Every person who has mastered their craft, all started out not knowing anything about that skill what so ever. Think back to the first day of your first job. If you're a parent, think back to your first day home with your new baby. You were disoriented, lost and felt overwhelmed with all the mechanics of this new task! But, here's the thing. You survived, didn't you? After a few weeks at your new job, you were pretty comfortable with it. In fact, if you've been doing your job for any length of time, like most people, you can probably do it with your eyes shut. Skilled hockey players can avoid that punishing check and put the puck in the 5-hole without breaking a sweat. Skilled warehouse logistic people can do a perfect inventory count in minutes. A highly trained dentist can do a root cannel effortlessly. And anyone who's been a parent for more than a month, can change a diaper with one hand while texting their best friend and cooking dinner with the other!

The point is that you aren't an old dog trying to learn a new trick. Whatever age you are at, you have the ability to learn something new every day. And so you should! Whether it is to better yourself at work for that new promotion coming up, become closer with your partner, or learning the skill you need to start your own business... any time you can learn a new skill or trade, it immediately increases your value to those around you that you serve. Think about it.

Fry cooks at McDonald's only earn about $11 per hour because that's the value their boss feels that they offer. The CEO of any large company is earning at least a quarter million dollars a year. Why? Because the company owner feels that is what their value is worth. What about a high goal scoring NHL hockey player? If they are having a good season, it isn't uncommon for the team owner to pay them over a million dollars per year! Again, because in the eyes of team owner, that player is high in value due to the large crowds and profits he brings in!

Although I'm an advocate of lifelong learning, you have to be selective of what specific education you are learning. There are still a large number of people out there that are trapped in out of date thinking. Their philosophy is to go to school, study hard and get a good education. From there, you will go out and get a good job where you will work at for the next 40 or so years. Then you step into those retirement years and the company and government will support you with a healthy pension until your time on this planet earth expires. Well, that may have been sound advice some years back after the war. But now, we are living in a different time.

First of all, you'd be very hard pressed to find a company that would want to keep you on their pay roll for 40+ years. And second, I can't imagine staying with the same company for that long, doing basically the same job day in and day out, year after year. And worst of all, not seeing much of increase in your pay grade over those four decades! Corporate America is all about the bottom line. **Their** bottom line! I'm sorry to be the one that burst your bubble, but the good ol' days of job security are long gone. You are just a number to most companies these days, and if they need to trim the fat on their budget – YOU'RE IT! Your many years of loyal service and dedicated work mean nothing. If the company is looking to trim back $50,000 in expenses, and your salary is in that ballpark area... and you are not giving them equal or greater value than that.... Bye-bye!

The other side of this equation is why would you want to be doing the same mundane job, looking at the same four walls, and have to beg your boss for time off when your child is sick, and you have to stay home to take care of them? If you are working for a company, they tell you the hours you must work. They tell you how much money you will earn. They tell you if you get to take holidays, and if so, when you have to take your holidays. Who wants to give up that much freedom, while working so hard to make someone else wealthy?

You will often hear a negative buzz when someone in the 'network marketing' industry approaches you, full of excitement and claims that 'their company' is the best out there, and you will become a millionaire within your first 9 months in the company.

You're first thought will likely be 'Hmm. Sounds like a pyramid scheme to me... no thanks! I'll just stick with my 9-5 job!"

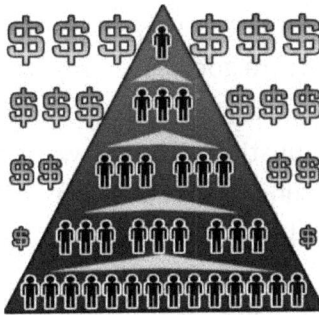

Let's consider that for a moment, shall we. Using the above photo as a guide, isn't it fair to say everyone working for Corporate America, or working for a mom and pop family business, or anyone that joins a health and wealth network marketing company, all are working under a 'pyramid scheme'? True, yes?

Those who start at an entry level position in any company, are earning less money and likely working harder than those above them. Those in middle management are earning more than those that are just starting out, and perhaps not working as hard. The owner or president of the company is earning much, much more than anyone else in the company. And, why shouldn't they?? It is their company, their risk, their equipment, their reputation and their dream that started the company in the first place!

Now you see the truth; that ALL businesses basically run as a 'pyramid scheme'. This may first hit you with a creepy feeling. But the reality is that for any business to run effectively and create a profit, that's how the pay structure goes. So, now that you understand the true outline of any business, you have to ask yourself an important question: Do you want to be a clog in the wheel, working hard to earn a healthy profit and comfortable living for the owner? Or do you want to be the owner of your own company, developing a strong and committed team beneath you, who will support you in a life of success, profit and comfort? To do this, you will first have to value your team and their contributions. Richard Branson, the CEO of Virgin Airlines reiterates this point.

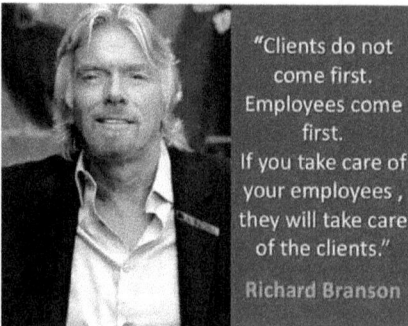

"Clients do not come first. Employees come first. If you take care of your employees, they will take care of the clients."

Richard Branson

Are you prepared to put in a few years of dedicated hard work for a life time of ease? Or are you someone that would rather stay stuck in the rat trap, making the top dog wealthy with your hard work?

Think about all the good that comes from you working for yourself. Your vision and mission planned out to bring out the best of all your clients. You are solving their problems, and going to bed feeling good about what you offer. You set your own hours. Initially, that may be 50 or 60 hours per week, or more. But once you get your business running with a system on auto pilot, those hours will get scaled down drastically. You work when you are most productive. For some people, the early bird catches the worm, and they are most productive in the early hours of the day, as the awakening sun welcomes them. Others like me, are more night hawks, and feel more productive at night. A large portion of this book was written in the later hours of the evening, after the wife and kids were asleep.

There are tax benefits of course, and no ceiling to the income you can earn. Do you want to bump up your sales next year by 20%? OK, go ahead and do it. You want to expand and go nationwide. Great, go for it!

If you are not yet in business for yourself, I'd highly encourage you to play with that idea. As we already discussed, you have a special talent inside you, which the world is waiting for you to share. The rewards far outweigh the false security you may feel by working for someone else. It is very unlikely that you will ever reach financial freedom by working for someone else. All you are really doing is bringing **them** closer to *their* financial and business goals!

AH-HA NOTES!

_____

_____

_____

_____

_____

_____

_____

_____

_____

_____

_____

_____

_____

_____

Step 7: **Yearn** the Reward

(DO DAILY™)

"All work and no play, makes Jack a dull boy!"

-proverb

Congratulations! You have written out your goals using the SMART goals template, and by following the DO DAILY™ steps outlined in previous chapters, you are well on your way to reaching that big goal. Keep in mind, before you picked up this book and started to apply my 7-step formula, your goals were no more than a distant dream that had little, if any, chance of ever coming to existence! You rolled up your sleeves, did the hard work that had to be done, and executed the plan! Reach over your shoulder and give yourself a well deserved pat on the back. Nice work my friend!

With every step that brings you closer to reaching your big goal, I want you to celebrate proportionately! Seriously! Don't wait until you finally reach that hurdle of attaining your big goal, but rather, celebrate every small step along the way. If you don't celebrate your successful steps along the way, you will get frustrated

and quit. You have to celebrate and stay motivated to keep going by acknowledging how far you've come thus far! Keep plugging away until you reach your big goal!

This would be an ideal time to talk about the special ingredient to reaching your goals and becoming successful. Do you have any idea what this magical ingredient is? Give up? OK. I'll share it with you. The secret ingredient that all highly successful people know and practice regularly is GRATITUDE! Far too many people think their life sucks, and don't show any appreciation for what they have. When you have a true, deep respect and appreciation for the things that you currently have – then, and only then, will you be granted with more gifts coming into your life! You need a MANTRA, a chant that you can repeat, like a team going into a championship game.

Instead of saying, 'My old rust bucket of a car is a pile of junk'. Replace that thinking with, *"I'm so thankful that I have a reliable car that gets my family and I safely to our destination."*

Instead of saying, 'I wish I had a bigger house. This one is so small'. Replace it with, *"I'm so grateful this house protects my family and shields us from the harsh environments"*.

Rather than thinking, 'I really hate my job. My boss is such a jerk!' Change that thinking to, *"I'm so grateful that I have a job which brings in enough money to support and help take care of my family."*

You get the idea. You have to show appreciation and gratitude for all that you <u>currently</u> have in your life on a daily basis. Every morning when you wake up, the first words out of your mouth need to be *"Thank you Lord / Universe/ Creator for the wonderful life you have given me today!"* The more specific you are the better. Be thankful for your home, your car, your family, your health, your job or business. And here's the key. Your gratitude... it has to be genuine. Don't just say the words. You have to FEEL THEM! You will find that when you are genuinely grateful for all you have in your life, then you will see more of what you want manifest into your life with ease! Here is the kicker. If you want to see good things happen twice as fast, just double up your efforts. Say your gratitude again before going to bed, and you will see wonderful things come into your life faster than you can imagine!

OK, let's get back to that celebrating of how far you've come thus far! I don't want you to skim over the accomplishments you've reached so far on the journey to reaching your goals. Be proud of what you've reached so far. You are so far ahead of where you were before you committed to going for your goals. Put it in your schedule, celebrate and embrace your goals reached thus far!

Sometimes, people feel that they don't deserve to give themselves a vacation, or perhaps they can't afford to take a vacation every year. Or even better, multiple vacations every year! My mentor takes a one week vacation <u>every month!</u> What?!? That can't be! When I first heard that, I couldn't believe it either. I mean who can afford a one week vacation every month? Really… how many people do you know that even get 12 WEEKS OF VACATION EACH AND EVERY YEAR?? Even if you got 12 weeks of vacation time every year, how the heck could you afford it, right?!? Here is his trick that I soon learned, and I'd highly suggest you start to practice this formula.

My mentor wasn't taking those vacations because he could afford it (both in time and financially). He took those vacations because every time he took a week vacation, he came back revitalized and pumped to take his business up another notch! Here is the secret trick I'd suggest you implement now. The truth is that when you first start this practice of taking 12, 1-week vacations per year, you most likely won't have 12 weeks of vacation time nor the finances to pay for 12 weeks of relaxing!

BUT…. What if, instead of taking a true 7 day vacation in a tropical resort or wherever you'd like… you took a mini vacation and treated it <u>exactly like it was a fully fledged **real** vacation</u>?

When my wife and I first started doing this, I was blown away at how amazing it made you feel! Our one week vacation (*in my mind*) was a trip to the Atlantis. We went scuba diving and saw exotic fish and sharks. We ate the most amazing food, and had so much fun. We took great pictures and did silly crazy things! It was awesome! Now, Remember, this is the vacation I convinced my mind that we were taking- not the actual vacation that we did.

In reality, this is how it played out. I found a discount voucher for $50 off the price of a meal at the Keg. I took my family there for my wife's birthday celebration, and we had a fantastic meal! I even talked the cute waiter into bringing out a piece of birthday cake and kissing my wife on the cheek. Once we were done the wonderful dinner, we walked a few blocks over to Ripley's Aquarium. Again, I was able to find discount vouchers for the family admittance. This place was fantastic! You walked through the glass tunnels, and just about every kind of water creature you can imagine swam over your head and around your body.

We took a bunch of pictures, did silly fun things, and in short, we had a fabulous "One week vacation!" So, let's compare a real vacation to our "Mind-Set vacation":

- **Real 1-Week Vacation**
- **Mind-Set 1-Week vacation**

Cost: *I'd guess about $8 - $10 thousand
** Less than $200

Time: *1 week, less travel time
= 5 vacation days
**One Friday evening

Good Memories: * maybe 8 out of 10
** 9 out of 10 for sure!

Recharged Energy: * Probably
** Absolutely!

Can you do this? Of course! A little bit of planning, and the right mindset that you will have a wonderful "1 week vacation" is all you will need! The way I see it, you can continue with your current plan of scrimping, saving, and begging your boss for some vacation time... and in 3 years from now MAYBE be lucky enough to have six or nine weeks of a superficial vacation.

My way of doing it, gives you **36** wonderful, amazing and memorable vacations by this time three years down the road. And, here's the icing on the cake. By training your mind to understand that you deserve to have as many amazing vacations as possible—pretty soon those pretend mini vacations, will be the real deal! You will actually be sitting on the beach drinking those cocktails with cute little umbrellas in them! BOO-YA! Go do this my friend... I promise you will thank me later for suggesting it!

Often, people don't want to do what has to be done to reach their big goals because they can't handle stepping out of their comfort zone. But think about that for a moment. Isn't the underlying reason why you want to set and reach goals, because you want to bring more abundance and success into your life? Which is more comfortable? Your current life of going to a job you don't really like, earning lower income than you deserve, living in a body that your aren't proud of, and seeing other successful people reaching their goals! The flip side of course, is doing the things that you may not like at the moment, but you knowing deep in your heart that a little bit of discomfort now, will bring you a lifetime of comfort afterwards! Doesn't it make sense to get comfortable with being uncomfortable while you reach your goals? The rewards are precious.

AH-HA NOTES!

_____

_____

_____

_____

_____

_____

_____

_____

_____

_____

_____

_____

_____

_____

_____

BRINGING IT ALL TOGETHER!

Congratulations.... You made it! If you've gotten this far, I'm going to assume you rolled up your sleeves and followed the seven step formula of reaching your goals. Look in the mirror and give yourself a thumb up!

It's one thing to read a book on theory, but I think the icing on the cake is to bring it all together through an example of someone going through the steps of setting a goal, and following the formula in this book to manifesting their big magnificent goal. Let's walk through the formula from start to finish!

OK, let's pick a fictional character who wants to write a personal development book on, oh I don't know, how about a great book on how to set and reach your goals using a simple formula. Let's call this character "Pauline". *Pauline* is a smart, ambitious person who dedicates her mission to helping people break their thinking that they won't ever be able to reach their goals.

Alright, as you recall, for any goal to even stand a chance of maturing, the first step is to get it out of your head, and down on paper. You want to be sure to use the SMART technique, remember? (Specific, Measurable, Attainable, Realistic, and Timely).

Here is *Pauline's* goal; ***"Someday I'd like to write a book. Not sure what kind of book yet, but that's what I want to do!"***

Does this goal fit into the SMART technique at all? No, not really. Let's try it again, shall we?

"My goal is to write a non-fiction personal development book on goal setting. I will write one chapter every two days for the next three months until the book is written. I will get help from my mentor(s), and be prepared to do whatever I have to, in order to get it completed!"

Let's test this goal. Does it fall into the SMART template? Specific- Yes, Measurable- Yes, Attainable- Yes, Realistic- Yes, Timely- Yes! Excellent! *Pauline* is now ready to harvest this goal to actually happening.

What will be *Pauline's* first step? Well, now that her goal is written down, she will want to post it somewhere that she can see and review it every day when she wakes up. I'd suggest the kitchen fridge or the bathroom mirror. To get her mind trained that she will actually reach this goal, she will read it out every morning when first awakening. When she reads it, it will be read with full emotion. She will read her goal of writing that book, as though it is already done!

Pauline knows that this is a big goal, and she will not be able to finish it on her own. She will have to enlist a support team to help her get it done {Delegate}. She gets herself a great mentor. She needs someone who is a master at reaching goals themselves, and has written a few books already. In fact, she picks a mentor who has written eight books, and offers a course on the exact steps you need to a write a book from start to finish!

Pauline knows that she has an inner gift that needs to be shared with the world {Offer Help}. Pauline has attended a number of seminars, and been a student of personal growth for a number of years. She knows there are far too many people out there that feel trapped, and can be doing better. She knows in her heart, that writing a book would be a great way to share her inner gift with the world.

There are days that *Pauline* feels stuck in getting the great content out of her head, onto paper. As she sits at her laptop, and looks around at the piles of clutter around her, she realizes the messes in her life are actually killing her inspiration. She decides to take the advice of her mentor, and clean up the messes, both externally, and the mental blocks as well {De-clutter}.

Although *Pauline* has been studying ways for people to improve their lives for a long time, why is it that she never followed the great advice of motivational speaker Zig Ziglar? He says that when you help enough people get what they want, you will be able to get what you want. *Pauline* realizes that Zig is a wise man and decides to share her message with the world. She commits to standing on her soap box and sharing all that she has learned in personal growth, with the world. She knows the great feeling she gets by helping others, will come back and reward her tenfold {Apply Knowledge}

To keep herself motivated to finish the book, *Pauline* decides it would be more productive to focus on the end reward of having completed that goal of writing a book, rather the tasks needed to get there! She pictures giving great talks and coaching to her eager students. Their lives are turning for the better, as is *Pauline's! {Increase Happiness}*

Although *Pauline* has hit her goal of getting her book done, she doesn't quit there. She knows that there are so many other avenues that she can help people turn their life around for the better. *Pauline* will continue her learning from her mentors, and share her teachings to her students in a clear way they understand {Learn Something New}

Wow! It's done! *Pauline* has written out her goals using the SMART technique, and has applied the DO DAILY™ formula, and thus has reached one of her big goals. She has celebrated the small steps along the way, such as finishing each chapter. And now, *Pauline* will celebrate her success in a big way {Yearn the Reward}. Maybe she will take her family to Atlantis to swim with the dolphins... or maybe she will just celebrate through a 'mini vacation' that you learnt in this book.

The goal cycle is now complete. Or is it? Actually no, it isn't. This particular goal is done, but there is so much more you want to achieve in your life. You have set your goal, and followed the simple 7-step formula to make sure you reach your goal. Now, you simply rinse and repeat.

What is your next big goal? Great! Write it down using the SMART technique and plug in the DO DAILY™ formula. Within a very short time, you will see that goal manifest into reality as well. Will you feel the fear at times? Absolutely! Here's the key. Yes, you will feel the fear at times through your journey. I'm asking you to break through that fear and do it anyways. A small bit of feeling uncomfortable initially, will actually make you feel quite comfortable for the rest of your life! It's time to "Go for the Goal'D™!!"

<u>AH-HA NOTES!</u>

_____

_____

_____

_____

_____

_____

_____

_____

_____

_____

_____

_____

_____

_____

_____

Paul's Recommended Books to Read

- ✓ *Think and Grow Rich*
  Napoleon Hill

- ✓ *The Science of Getting Rich*
  Wallace Wattles

- ✓ *Secrets of Millionaire Mind*
  T Harv Eker

- ✓ *The Success Principles*
  Jack Canfield

- ✓ *Double Your Income Doing What you Love*
  Raymond Aaron

- ✓ *Stop Whining and Start Winning*
  Paul Trottier

- ✓ *Yes! Energy*
  Loral Langemeier

- ✓ *Unleash the Power Within*
  Tony Robbins

BONUS CHAPTER

If you've made it this far through the book, then congratulations! There isn't a goal out there that you can't achieve! You now know that when you change your our mind set to that of one of belief, and use the DO DAILY™ formula as a template for your goals, then there isn't any goal you cannot manifest! There's no need to read any further. The next few pages, although may seem a bit whoo-whoo for some of you, is actually the magic ingredient I use in my life daily.   I call it the secret sauce of my success. It's the glue that turns my dreams into reality right before my eyes.

~~~~~~

Are you still with me? Fantastic! Thank you for putting your trust in me up to this point. As you may have realized while you were reading through this book, the biggest thing that stops most people from reaching their goals is that they are frozen with fear. They are fearful of how others will view them once they reach their goals. They are fearful of what others will think if they don't reach their goals. They are fearful that they may stumble along the way of going for their goals and fall on their face.

Guess what? No matter how well you lay out the plan for flawless journey to reaching your goal, you are going to have bumps along the way. Many people will say "I know there are goal dreams in my head that I want to achieve, but I don't know the steps to get there!" Please don't ever get snagged up with the *how to* of reaching your goals. As long as you have a rock solid belief in the pit of your stomach that you will reach your goal, the 'how' will always be outlined for you! Always!

I'm sure you have heard of the law of attraction which became a world-wide phenomenon during the hit movie and book, *The Secret,* which came out nearly a decade ago. In short the law of attraction states that like attracts like. This means that if you think you will never have a certain thing in your life, or you will never reach a certain goal, then you're right. You won't! If believe that you will reach certain goals and bounty into your life, then yes, you absolutely will!

Although *The Secret* gives you a good basis for setting and reaching your goals, it never really drills down to the true meat of the law of attraction. It gives the impression that if you just wish and hope for a million dollars or a new sports car... that those things will just magically fall out of the sky, onto your lap. You may have tried this practice yourself. How's that working for you? I'm guessing NOT WELL!

Perhaps wishing and hoping for abundance to happen in your life is the right intention, but there is much more to it than that. In fact, have you ever just wished, hoped for or dreamed of something good to happen in your life, and it did? I promise you it hasn't! If you answered yes to that question, that just means you did more than wish and hope for things to magically happen in your life. You had unwavering faith it would happen, and you took purposeful steps to reaching those goals and dreams.

There was a time not so long ago, when I was trapped in the corporate world, and was forced to do the back and forth long commute to work. In order to support my family, I had no choice but to get up early and fight traffic for an hour or more to get to work. I would put in my eight or nine hours at work, and then prepare for the stressful fight in traffic to get back home at the end of the day. It was exhausting and was draining me physically, mentally and spiritually! I was out of the house and away from my family for over 12+ hours a day. I knew there just had to be a better option.

I vividly remember a Wednesday evening, coming home one night, and the traffic was at a snail's pace. I kept getting more angry and frustrated, as I knew I had to get home to pick up my boys and get them to parade inspection for the cadet program they were in. I felt like I was letting them down. I threw my hands up in the air and prayed in desperation. *"GOD, I don't have the power to change this. Doing this daily commute is draining me, putting a strain on my marriage and my relationships with my children. I can NOT fight this any longer! I put 100% of my faith in you LORD, to change my path and help me with this heavy burden in my life! You have the power. Please help me!"*

I spent the last sixteen years of my career fighting this demon on my own. It seemed, no matter what I did, I could not escape the torturous daily commute to and from work! The minute I released it all to GOD, I felt like a thousand pound weight was lifted off my chest! Immediately after I asked my LORD to help me, things turned for the better. The traffic seemed to effortlessly open up, and I made it home shortly thereafter to get my boys to cadets with time to spare.

The traffic clearing up was only the tip of the iceberg! Less than two weeks later, the universe performed the most amazing miracle that I could have ever imagined. This is how fast it happened, and I was totally blown away. As I mentioned, it was a Wednesday evening that I prayed and asked GOD to help me. Two days later, we got notice at work that the vice president was being let go. No one expected this sudden move at all. It caught most of the staff by surprise. This vice president was an 'old school' thinker, and wasn't even open to the idea of me working from home. Not one day a week... certainly not five days a week! By noon that Friday, the vice president was walked off the property, and I never saw him again.

The following Monday, the brand new vice president came in, and went around to each office to introduce himself to the team. He seemed keen to get to know his team and unitize our strengths to turn the company around for the better. I gave him a brief overview of what specifically I did, and which account I managed. I was part of a team that managed the biggest account for my employer.

Later that same day, we got another surprise notice. The team lead for one of our east coast branches was leaving, by the end of the week, and her replacement backup had very little training with the account I was managing. Normally she would be expected to give two weeks' notice, but her new employer did not want to wait that long. Our brand new vice president was forced to make his first big decision only hours after taking his new seat as head of the company.

He called an emergency meeting Monday afternoon, with the aim of how to handle this short notice from the St John's branch. The new VP quickly realized that this was our biggest account, and he needed to have someone there quickly to ensure a smooth transaction with the less experienced person that would be filling this new role. It was decided that I'd be the best fit to fly to the St John's office to train this new person and get him up to speed. The following morning, I was on a plane to the east coast to make sure this new person would be properly trained and adopted into his new role. I trained this new person for the rest of the week, and just before boarding my Friday afternoon flight back to Ontario, my new VP called me. He wanted to have a quick debriefing Monday morning, to bring him up to speed with the training I had been doing all week long.

Monday morning I headed to the new VP's office to discuss our options with this new person to fill such a big role.

"So, tell me Paul, how did the training go with the new guy in the east coast?"

'Not really any issues boss. He's bright, learns quickly and seems eager to run a smooth branch. I got him all set up with his login passwords and made sure he was trained on the day to day duties and expectations. My only suggestion would be to have someone login remotely in the morning to keep an eye on the branch.'

"Yes, that's a good idea, Paul. Is that something we can actually do?"

'It sure is, Wayne.' I replied. 'In fact, I'd be happy to monitor that branch to make sure we don't have any surprises. There is one small problem with that idea, however.'

"Oh, what would that be?" the VP questioned.

'Well Wayne…. With it being our most eastern branch, their start time of 8am is actually 6:30am here in Ontario. Now, I don't have a problem doing that, but I do have a problem leaving my house at 5:30am to be here for 6:30am to login and monitor that branch!'

"Humm.. I see." said the VP thoughtfully.

'I do have a plan though, if you are open to it.' I explained.

"Go on…" Wayne said with interest.

'Well, I'm quite fine to login this early to monitor this branch, but there really is no need for me to leave my home to do this. In fact, as long as I have internet connection and a phone, I can do my job from anywhere in the world!'

"I see… and what about your reporting manager and team here? How would that work?"

'Actually Wayne… I only work with one other fellow. In fact, <u>he also works out of his home in Winnipeg</u>, and covers the west coast branches. I work here in Ontario, and cover the east coast branches."

The new VP paused for a moment before replying.

"Well, I'm OK with you working from home, just as long as the customer service does not drop."

What?!? I couldn't believe my ears! The very next day (less than 2 weeks after my plea to GOD), I was working out of the comfort of my home, and have never had to do that horrible drive again!

Now, let's analyze this for a moment. Over sixteen years of trying to figure this out on my own, with nothing but frustration and stress for so many years. There is absolutely no possible way any of this could have happened without GOD doing his miracles in the background BEFORE I even asked for his help!

For the old VP to be fired on the Friday (two days after my plea), and the new VP to start on the following Monday... there would have had to been extensive talks going on between the company owner and the new VP at least three or four weeks prior to him starting.

What about the lady in the east coast branch that quit. She was obviously looking for work maybe a month or more prior to her giving notice that she was leaving. Why did she only give one week notice, rather than the normal two week notice? Why was I the one selected to fly there and train this new person? They could have sent any other of a half a dozen people. Why did the conversation between me and the new vice president go the way it did? Why did I suggest the plan of monitoring that branch from home? I didn't even think of that until the words came out of my mouth! What did I just say to this guy?? Why was the new VP so open to my plan?

WOW. That whole process just took my breath away and left me in awe! I talk in previous chapters of the importance of having a strong support team to help you reach your goals. Do you know who I consider to be my first and foremost support team member? I tell you this... there is no way what so ever, that I'd ever be able to reach any of my goals without 100% faith that my creator is there beside me to ensure I can tackle any goal I set my sights on!

You may or may not be a believer of God. That's OK. Perhaps, you have a different name for you creator. All I can share with you is that my spiritual belief has helped me to do things I never dreamed possible! I know that as soon as my faith drops even slightly, the path to my goal becomes much tougher! I believe, and take a small step towards my goals, and GOD takes a huge leap in bringing me closer to my goals. I'm granted with more favor into my life. When my belief drops ever so slightly and I take a small step <u>away</u> from my goals, then GOD takes a huge leap away! Strong faith brings me to my goals faster and easier. Why would I possibly try to do it on my own? I leave you with this little poem of faith. You may have heard it.

Footprints in the Sand, a beautiful poem!

One night I dreamed a dream.
I was walking along the beach with my Lord.
Across the dark sky flashed scenes from my life.
For each scene, I noticed two sets of footprints in the sand,
One belonging to me and one to my Lord.

After the last scene of my life flashed before me,
I looked back at the footprints in the sand.
I noticed that at many times along the path of my life,
especially at the very lowest and saddest times,
there was only one set of footprints.

This really troubled me, so I asked the Lord about it.
"Lord, you said once I decided to follow you,
You'd walk with me all the way.
But I noticed that during the saddest and most troublesome
times of my life,
there was only one set of footprints.
I don't understand why, when I needed You the most, You
would leave me."

He whispered, "My precious child, I love you and will never leave
you
Never, ever, during your trials and testing's
When you saw only one set of footprints,
It was then that I carried you."

- By Mary Stevenson

AH-HA NOTES!

_____

_____

_____

_____

_____

_____

_____

_____

_____

_____

_____

_____

_____

_____

About the Author

Paul C Trottier, known by many as the "Getting the GOAL'D"™ Coach, is an award winning author who specializes in helping authors, entrepreneurs and those with a big goal; break past their fear barriers, and tackle their largest dreams with a head-on game plan!

His intensive courses, speaking engagements, goal achievement seminars and personal 1 on 1 mentoring, has inspired individuals to take their lives to their fullest potential! Paul's personal goal is to make a positive contribution to the lives of millions and he is passionate about helping others to achieve their goals.

Please visit Paul's website; www.startwinningcoach.com for bonus materials and how to connect with him!